D0875603

NEW FRONTIERS
FOR PROFESSIONAL
MANAGERS

MCKINSEY FOUNDATION LECTURE SERIES

Sponsored by the
Graduate School of Business, Columbia University

NEW FRONTIERS
FOR PROFESSIONAL
MANAGERS

RALPH J. CORDINER
President, General Electric Company

McGraw-Hill Book Company, Inc.
New York   Toronto   London   1956

IV

PREFACE

Our modern society is characterized by large organizations. Their effective and democratic management is of vital concern to all of us. Particularly in the field of business, the importance of achieving the efficient voluntary association of men and women in large and rapidly growing corporations gives a new and perhaps unexpected significance to the subject of the management of large organizations.

Aware of this significance, the McKinsey Foundation for Management Research, Inc., founded and supported by the partners of the management consulting firm of McKinsey & Company, made an initial grant to the Graduate School of Business to organize and sponsor a continuing series of distinguished lectures by men of conspicuous accom-

v

plishment in the management of large organizations. The reflections and thoughts of men of action, often too busy to organize and place on paper the rich usefulness of their experience, will thus be made available to present and future students of management.

In inaugurating the McKinsey Foundation Lecture Series at the Graduate School of Business, Columbia University, we were fortunate to be able to present one of the most thoughtful and effective of our contemporary business executives, who gave us a close-up picture of his approach to the problems of managing a large organization. This kind of authoritative interpretation of modern management methods is close to the heart of a real understanding of the American business system.

Mr. Ralph J. Cordiner, President of the General Electric Company, as the first McKinsey lecturer, afforded our students, our faculty, and our distinguished guests from the business community an intimate interpretation of his and his associates' managerial philosophy. His prompt grasp of the real spirit of the lectures can perhaps be best described in his own words:

"As I understand it, one of the purposes of the lectures is to coax us businessmen out of our offices and into the arena of public thought where our managerial philosophies can be put to the test of examination by men trained in other disciplines. At the same time, it is hoped that in describing our personal experiences in managing today's corporations we will help bridge the disturbing gap between academic theory and the living realities of the new American economy.

"Within our own country, the lag between theory and practice is reflected in wasteful frictions and antagonisms between government, business, unions, education and other institutions. Because of the national obsession with concepts that are no longer relevant—concepts of Old World capitalism and Old World socialism—each of these groups finds much of its own work frustrated or attacked on the basis of wholly obsolete assumptions as to the nature of economic life in the United States today.

"This situation is increasingly recognized by educators, businessmen, and other informed people. It will require the efforts of all to bring an adequate resolution. If the McKinsey Lectures can help in this process of reducing the gap between economic theory and practice, they can make an important contribution to our national life."

These lectures provide one of the ways in which the Graduate School of Business expects to respond to this opportunity to achieve a perceptive and accurate interpretation of the American business system.

The initial lectures were presented to a group of prominent businessmen and scholars on the Columbia campus and are now made available to a wider audience through the publication of this volume. The lectures are reproduced here substantially as they were given, in three parts, during late April and early May, 1956. With the editorial assistance of Professor James W. Kuhn of the Graduate School of Business and Mr. Robert L. Fegley of the General Electric Company, some additional material has been added from the tape recording of Mr. Cordiner's responses to questions and problems raised in the after-dinner discussions which followed each lecture.

> COURTNEY C. BROWN
> *Dean*
> *Graduate School of Business*
> *Columbia University*

June, 1956

CONTENTS

NEW FRONTIERS

FOR PROFESSIONAL

MANAGERS

NEW
CORPORATE
DIMENSIONS

Many thoughtful persons have observed that the United States has evolved a wholly new form of capitalism, variously called democratic capitalism, mass capitalism, or—more aptly—people's capitalism. As the first nation in the world to break through the ancient barriers of scarcity into an economy of abundance, we have a unique experience that we ourselves need fully to understand and to communicate to the rest of the world. But somehow we have not yet been able to do it well—to describe this new people's capitalism, and all that it means to the spiritual and cultural life of the people, as well as to their material well-being.

At a time when many nations of the world are just beginning to industrialize, and when our leadership is most needed, such a weakness can have tragic and historic consequences.

Within our own country, the lag between theory and practice is reflected in wasteful frictions and antagonisms between government, business, unions, education, and other institutions. Because of the national obsession with concepts that are no longer relevant—concepts of old world capitalism and old world socialism—each of these groups finds much of its own work frustrated or attacked on the basis of wholly obsolete assumptions as to the nature of economic life in the United States today.

This situation is increasingly recognized by educators, businessmen, and other informed people. It will require the efforts of all to bring an adequate resolution. The McKinsey Lectures, by recording the experiences and philosophies of men engaged in the management of large enterprises, may be helpful in reducing the gap between economic theory and practice.

Let us begin with some commentary on the rise of large-scale economic enterprises.

Whenever a society industrializes, one of the most important characteristics is a great increase in the scale of its undertakings. The drive toward more complex technologies, toward more massive use and guidance of the forces of nature, toward mass production and mass distribution, necessarily results in the development of large-scale economic organizations. England has them, Russia has them, Germany has them, other industrial nations have them, and the United States has them. Their size is generally related to the size and technical capacity of the national economy in which they operate. Without these large-scale economic enterprises, a nation today is a second-rate power and its people suffer both lower standards of living and greater vulnerability to attack by aggressive nations.

In the United States, with its deep dedication to human liberty and its competitive economic system, the characteristic form for these large-scale economic enterprises is the modern corporation, of which General Electric is an example. In other countries, with other traditions, they may take the form of state-owned or state-regulated organizations, with all that is implied in terms of state control of the life and work of the citizens. In Russia, for example, we see the strange distortion of a state which can produce thermonuclear explosions and advanced jet aircraft, yet is unwilling to provide enough bread, shoes, and housing for its people. It appears that freedom is required to assure that these large enterprises will serve the people most effectively.

The modern American corporation certainly poses problems of its own, both social and political. But on balance, most observers agree that it has delivered the goods more abundantly than any visible alternative anywhere in the world.

When I say delivered the goods, I mean that the people have in their hands, not promises, but an abundance of the material things that are desired by this country's citizens. As a consequence of this abundance, people in the United States have awakened to new opportunities for cultural and spiritual attainment, new dimensions of freedom, that become possible in an economy where the basic physical needs can be taken almost for granted.

ROLE OF LARGE ENTERPRISES

Because these lectures deal specifically with the management of *large* enterprises, it might be worthwhile to summarize, briefly, their role in our national life. It is a creative role which might be characterized in three points:

First, the large enterprise is a source of innovation. It operates on a scale large enough to afford the staff of managers, scientists, engineers, production men, marketing men, employee and public relations men, financial men, and other functional specialists required to create—continuously—new knowledge, new products, and new markets. Out of these innovations come that stream of new industries which we take almost for granted these days, the new industries that provide fresh business opportunity for small and large companies and provide employment for our expanding population.

Second, the large enterprise is a source of mass production and mass distribution. It has the capacity to take new-product ideas out of the research and engineering laboratory and, in a relatively short time, make them generally available to the people. Here again, it is important to remember that smaller companies always do much of the work involved in processing materials, making components, providing supplies and services, performing sales and distribution functions, and carrying on other profitable portions of the over-all business flow. But generally it is the large enterprise that energizes the great flow of work involved in serving a mass market. Without the human and material resources of the large enterprise, and its ability to take large, long-term risks, these mass-production and mass-distribution processes simply would not get started and probably would not even continue to operate successfully.

Third, the large enterprise is a source of advanced

technical capacity. It is the developer, designer, producer, and distributor of the complex, advanced products and systems of our age: the turbines, the atomic-power reactors, and even the advanced defense-weapons systems that cannot be produced with limited resources either of men or facilities.

One might add other categories in describing the role of the large enterprise, but these three—innovation, mass production and distribution, and advanced technical capacity—indicate how the large enterprise serves as an energizer of business activity. It sets up a dynamic flow of work and money which moves swiftly through the nation's highly integrated economy and provides much of its living, expansive power.

I have spoken in terms of the large manufacturing company, but the description applies with equal force to the large financial and service institutions, the large power-supply and transportation enterprises, or any other large economic organization. The large enterprises provide innovation, mass service, and advanced technical capacity.

This is not the place to take up the distinctive contributions of other segments of the economy— the smaller enterprises, the professions, universities and colleges, the unions, the government, and others. But it is important to see their interdependence, each relying on the other to perform some necessary function in getting the nation's work accomplished.

The purpose of this prologue on the nature and function of large enterprises has been to indicate why it is in the public interest that the large corporations continue to be expertly, profitably, and responsibly managed. They are business enterprises. They must serve, survive, and grow in a competitive business system. They must therefore make healthy profits, as an incentive to investors to risk their savings, and as a resource for the forward-driving work of innovation which provides so much of the vitality of our expanding economy.

Now let us consider the particular subject of this discourse, the General Electric Company.

CHARACTERISTICS OF
GENERAL ELECTRIC

Although there are many similarities among leading modern companies, there are also differences. Each of them has distinctive characteristics and even distinctive "personality." In this first lecture, I should like to give you a rather detailed description of the General Electric Company—a popularly owned, highly diversified Company which has long been essentially growing from within rather than by purchasing and merger. It is a Company whose antecedents go back 77 years—and it is still a "growth" Company. It is important that you have a picture in depth of the Company because the opportunities and problems of its management arise from the very nature of the enterprise and its environment.

General Electric is an American manufacturing company which is devoted first to serving the United States market, though it also serves a world market that is hungry for electrical and related products. The environment which nurtured this Company, therefore, is the exuberantly expansive economy of the United States, in which spectacular growth and perpetual change are normal, healthy characteristics.

The beginnings of General Electric date back to October, 1878, when a group of investors joined together to finance Thomas Edison's experiments with the incandescent lamp. That is to say, the original Company was formed to finance innovation. This emphasis on innovation has remained a hallmark of the Company since that time. In 1892, a number of pioneer companies in the electrical field incorporated as the General Electric Company, with headquarters at the former Edison General Electric Company in Schenectady, New York.

In the time between the founding of the Company and now, the United States has grown tremendously. Not only has population increased from 66 million to the present figure of 168 million, but the economy has also become enormously more productive. Whereas in 1900 the United States produced about $75 billion in goods and services (in terms of 1956 dollars), this year it will produce about $406 billions. In this period there were two great wars in which the country was obliged to exert every ounce of productive strength in order to turn back the forces of aggression. These wars gave us a new vision of what we could do, in terms of production, and provided a tremendous psychological stimulus for increased peacetime living standards.

It was in the resultant stimulating, expansive, electrifying environment that General Electric grew in service to the nation. It grew essentially because it was able to provide what the people wanted, in the form of products and services, and because electric power is at the very heart of the American economy and national security.

LEADING ELECTRICAL MANUFACTURER

The first prominent characteristic of this Company, therefore, is that it is the leading manufacturer in the electrical industry. General Electric was formed when the United States began to turn from muscle power to electric power. If you think of the consequences of that statement, you will realize that General Electric was fortunate to enter the most dramatic and sustained growth business of the twentieth century.

Electric service for cities, for homes, for farms, for stores and offices, for factories, for transportation, for communication, for entertainment, and for national defense: The multiplication of the use of electricity in America since the "dark ages" only 50 years ago is an event of radical significance in human history. Statistically, the use of electricity has doubled every decade since the 1880's and has grown three times as fast as the nation's economy. To my knowledge, no other industry can show such sustained progress. But the astonishing thing is that, instead of tapering off after 70 years, the pace of electrification is actually accelerating. The United States is now doubling its use of electrical energy every eight years. After 70 years of headlong expansion, the electrical industry is growing faster than ever.

To understand the role of the manufacturer in this growth, one has to recognize what we call "the benign circle of electric power." A turbine-generator installed in a power station makes possible the sale of more lamps, appliances, motors, and other users of power. And as more people buy lamps, appliances, and so on, they create the need for another turbine-generator and more transmission equipment. Thus each new use of electricity accelerates the turn of the circle—creating a bigger potential market for General Electric products, not only in end-use customer equipment, but in equipment to produce, transmit, and distribute electric power.

Because of this, we have found that the most directly measurable yardstick for the Company's growth, past and future, is the growth curve of the use of electricity in the United States. Our forecasts indicate that the use of electricity will double in the next eight to ten years, and probably quadruple in the next sixteen years. From this you can draw your own conclusions as to the opportunities for everyone in the electrical manufacturing industry. With the possible exception of the petro-chemical industry, this is the fastest growing major industry in the nation.

WIDESPREAD POPULAR OWNERSHIP

The second prominent characteristic of General

11

Electric is its widespread popular ownership. It is appropriate that this Company, whose products are used by practically every family in the United States, and which is so important to our country's future growth, is also owned by the people.

Today, there are 358,000 owners of General Electric, more than half of them women. Nearly 13,000 institutions, such as pension funds, schools, and churches, own shares in General Electric. No one individual owns as much as one tenth of one percent of the shares outstanding. Although AT&T and General Motors have more share owners, we seem to be a highly popular investment for the small investor. Today, more people are investing in General Electric stock through the Stock Exchange's Monthly Investment Plans than any other stock.

Another significant trend is that General Electric's employees are becoming owners of the Company. Today, more than 50,000 General Electric employees are share owners in the Company, and 65,000 more are becoming owners through the Company's Savings and Stock Bonus Plan. This group of employee-share owners represents approximately one half of the employees.

Here, it seems to me, is convincing evidence that the "people's capitalism" is a living fact. Through life insurance and other financial institutions, practically everybody in the country participates in the ownership of industry. More importantly, the number of persons who hold shares of stock directly is increasing steadily, from 6 million people in 1951 to 8 million at present, and the New York Stock Exchange predicts the figure will be around 13 million people by 1965. In my opinion, we should aim for even broader share ownership.

In the next ten years, industry is going to require from 400 to 500 billion dollars to replace and expand its plant and equipment. If an increasing portion of this capital can be obtained from the great middle-income groups, we will not only tap a fresh source for financing the country's future, but more citizens will have a visible share in its economic strength. The aim of people's capitalism should be to make as many citizens as possible triple participants in the national economy—as customers, producers, and share owners.

The share owners in General Electric expect not only regular dividends, but gains in the value of their investment. In both respects, the Company's record has been good. In the 64 years since its incorporation, the Company has never failed to earn a profit; it has paid a dividend every year since 1899;

and it is considered one of the classical "growth companies."

One of the brokerage houses tells of a lady (they call her Miss Jones) who called their office and said, "I own about $600 worth of General Electric stock. Why is it that they pay me dividends lately of about $300 per year? Isn't that a pretty high income rate and don't you think they have made some mistake?"

The facts are that back in 1920, on Miss Jones' twenty-first birthday, her father purchased for her, as a present, five shares of General Electric common stock for which he told her he paid about $600. Apparently since then, Miss Jones has been steadfastly refusing to read any of the frequent and voluminous literature the Company mails to keep our share owners informed about their investment. Anyway, she was astonished to learn that, as a result of earnings re-invested in the Company, her $600 worth of stock is now worth more than $10,000. In addition, she has received more than $4,600 in cash dividends since 1920. So, an investment risk of about $600 thirty-four years ago is now worth well over $14,000 including the income.

At any time in those 34 years, Miss Jones could have taken her money out of General Electric and spent it, perhaps on those appliances we would like her to buy. But because she was willing to refrain from spending it on immediate consumption, and was willing to risk the chance that the Company would fail, not succeed, she has been handsomely rewarded and her money has helped to build up the Company's and the country's wealth-producing capacity.

To assure that the interests of the owners will be protected, General Electric share owners are represented by one of the finest Boards of Directors in the United States. These 19 men, of whom only two (the Chairman and myself) are members of the Company's management, are very diligent in their work as directors. They are highly representative in a geographical sense, which is appropriate for a Company whose activities are nation-wide. They are also representative in the sense of the wide variety of their experience in the business life of this country, which includes experience in education, food, agriculture, mining, manufacturing, marketing, banking and finance, and transportation. In addition, they represent a fine balance of the vigor of youth and the wisdom of long years of service. All in all, there is probably no more representative Board of Directors in the United States. It is obvious that a Board of such breadth and distinction is an additional assurance that the Company will serve not only the share owners, but the public interest.

PROFESSIONAL MANAGERS

As an important consequence of the Company's widespread popular ownership, we come to the next characteristic of General Electric; namely, that it is managed by professional managers. These managers, including myself, are not the owners of the business, but employees hired by the share owners through their elected directors to manage their business in the balanced best interests of all concerned. This separation of ownership and the managerial function—increasingly common in business today—has important consequences.

The work of managing is tending to become professional, as a distinct kind of work in itself. It is becoming a job that requires a great amount of specialized thought, effort, and training in the principles as well as the techniques of managing. For the manager has the challenging task of getting results through the work of other men and women, rather than directly by his own effort.

This professional approach requires, in fact, a dedication of the man's self and service not only to the owners of the business through his Board of Directors, but also as a steward to the Company's customers, its industry, its employees, and to the community at large. The professional manager must consciously place the balanced best interests of these ahead of his own personal interests. The corporate manager today thus has an opportunity and an obligation for service comparable to the highest traditions of any professions in the past.

TRADITION OF PUBLIC RESPONSIBILITY

This leads to the next characteristic of General Electric, which is a long tradition of public responsibility. Since its beginnings, General Electric has been led by men of the highest integrity. Charles Coffin, Edwin Rice, Gerard Swope, and Owen D. Young, our presidents and chairmen from 1892 to 1940, won high regard as business statesmen, although some of their pioneering doctrines with respect to employee and public responsibility were frequently regarded as radical in their time. The work of Charles E. Wilson and Philip D. Reed in the service of their country is well known, and most of us have had more than a taste of public service, particularly during the wartime emergencies.

General Electric people have tried to deserve and

maintain a reputation for integrity, warmth, and friendliness in their dealings with the public. This is reflected in practically all surveys of public opinion, which indicate that the public has a very high regard for the Company.

In the communities where we have manufacturing facilities and offices, it is the Company's policy to contribute and participate generously in community activities, and to encourage employees to lend their time and talents to local affairs. Because the Company is so deeply dependent on high levels of education in this country—to provide not only well-educated employees, but also well-educated consumers and fellow-citizens—General Electric has long had close relationships with the educational world. The Company's formal contributions to education this year, some through the General Electric Educational and Charitable Fund, will amount to $1,400,000, in scholarships, fellowships, and gifts to the colleges. In addition, the Company provides considerable assistance in the form of teaching aids and equipment.

There is no time to expand on the policy problems that are raised by the question of educational and charitable contributions, but they are deeply important. Regardless of how generous their motives may be, managers or directors have no legal right to distribute the share owners' money with lavish and irresponsible hand in order to satisfy some vaguely conceived public obligation.

A Company like General Electric has no magic or secret source of wealth, from which it can subsidize good works. It is actually a clearinghouse of economic activity. The Company collects money from its customers, at competitive prices, in return for products and services. All this money is in turn redistributed to employees, share owners, suppliers, and others in proportion to their respective contribution to the Company's results, and also to the government's tax collectors. To the degree that education and other community activities contribute to the success of the Company and the society in which it operates, they should and do receive a share of the proceeds.

The important principle I should like to express here, in relations with customers, share owners, employees, suppliers, educational institutions, charitable activities, government, and the general public, is that all activities must be guided by the recognition of common purposes and of the contribution that each group makes toward their achievement. Now, the modern corporation, particularly one which has such deep roots in the United States society as General Electric, is taking an increasingly enlightened view as to what such institutions as education actually provide, and what are the Company's consequent obligations. I am certain that business must do more, rather than less, to help higher education in the years ahead. But the guiding policy must be one of equal and reciprocal obligations, with complete respect for the independence and integrity of each party. With this view, a balanced view of the claims and contributions of all who affect the Company's operations, we have a sound guide toward meeting our responsibilities to society.

An important consideration in meeting a company's public responsibilities is participation in the national defense. Like most other companies, General Electric prefers commercial, non-defense business because it is generally more open for Company-determined innovations and is more profitable. But because of the Company's unique technical capacities, it is called upon regularly to develop and produce complicated equipment and systems for the armed forces. Today, defense business amounts to about 20% of General Electric's total volume and uses an even larger proportion of its technically trained people.

The Company's policy is to concentrate its efforts on those defense projects where it can make a distinctive technical contribution—generally the advanced scientific weapons systems and equipments, and the unsolved problems in military technology. As to the production aspects of the job, we subcontract important elements of the work to other companies, especially to able small companies which can bring special skills and flexibility to bear. It is evident that the United States will have to maintain a high degree of preparedness for years to come, with continually advancing technical requirements. Therefore substantial sums of the Company's money have been invested in developmental and production facilities for military equipment, and we expect to keep those facilities busy.

In defense work, in community and educational affairs, in serving the public interest, General Electric is constantly re-examining its responsibilities. As society changes, we are trying as hard as we know how to respond thoughtfully and creatively to the social responsibilities of a new age.

FOCUS ON THE CUSTOMER

General Electric is a customer-focused Company. We earnestly believe in the concept, "No Sale, No

Job." A company must avoid favoring any one group at the expense of the others, whether customers, share owners, employees, suppliers, or another group. But the need to attract and serve customers provides a common focus for the efforts of all of us.

This statement may seem like a pointless platitude, but it is astonishing how often managements make the error of letting the focus of the business fall on other groups.

Sometimes, for example, managers elect or are persuaded to run the business primarily for the "good" of the employees and will grant unwarranted wage increases or turn over managerial and share-owner prerogatives to union officials. In these cases, the costs of such "deals" are passed along to the customer, or result in ignoring some other group.

Frequently the management focuses excessively and short-sightedly on share-owner interests. Such a business is bound to deteriorate and lose its competitive position.

Or managements can become obsessed with their own perpetuation, acting as though they and their management associates were indispensable. They may develop a mistaken idea of what they call public service; or they may become subservient to retailers or distributors.

A business must be managed in the balanced best interests of all the groups who contribute to its success, but the efforts of all must be focused on the customer. If the customer is well served, share owners, employees, suppliers, dealers, and communities will all prosper.

Consider the lot of the average General Electric employee, as an example. General Electric is one of the major sources of employment in the United States. Since 1939 employment in the Company has been increasing at a rate six times as fast as in the country as a whole. Today, the Company is providing employment for 252,000 people in every state of the Union, plus 29,000 in foreign lands.

These are good positions—and they are improving. In 1939, the average General Electric employee earned $2,028 a year including the value of benefit programs. Today, a General Electric position is worth $5,627 a year, on the average, and that includes a splendid package of pension, insurance, vacation, holiday, and other benefits providing better economic security. As we introduce greater automation and the proportion of skilled workers increases, the average General Electric employee of 1965 may well be earning as high as $8,000 to $9,000 a year in pay and benefits.

From reading the headlines these days, one might assume that the so-called fringe benefits are a recent innovation in the business world. On the contrary, this Company and others pioneered many years ago in programs to provide for employment security. The General Electric Pension Plan was introduced in 1912 and has already paid out $150,000,000. Our insurance plans started in 1920 and many other benefit programs had their beginnings in that era. The Company is still pioneering. Last year there were 32 significant improvements in pay and benefits, including a medical insurance plan which is far ahead of any other medical insurance plan in industry, providing employees up to $15,000 insurance against the cost of catastrophic illnesses.

Over and above these obvious pay and security values, we are engaged in deep research into the really important values of human work: the spiritual satisfactions that come from a challenging position that brings a man or woman a sense of achievement, of belonging, of worthwhile personal expression.

This area of human motivations is an exciting frontier for modern industry, and is perhaps the ultimate challenge of the industrial society.

In this same area of human relations we must consider the suppliers, distributors, and retailers, who also share in the prosperity and growth of General Electric.

Since 1939, the Company's payments for materials, supplies, and services have increased more than 10 times. At the present time we have about 40,000 suppliers, most of them small businesses. The flow of business from General Electric to its suppliers amounted to nearly a billion and a half dollars in 1955, and there is no way to measure the consequent flow of business to their component and material suppliers, and so on through various supplying companies, large and small, that live by serving the ultimate customers for electrical products.

In addition, roughly 400,000 small companies gain all or part of their income from selling, installing, and servicing the Company's products.

General Electric's relationships with suppliers and dealers are designed to be personal, friendly, and mutually helpful. We depend on them and they depend on us in the flow of production and distribution. There are both legal and ethical considerations involved in relationships with these other companies. The primary principle here is to maintain a deep respect for their independence and integrity, and yet to achieve with them a sense of unity in serving our mutual end customers.

TECHNICAL SKILLS AND FACILITIES

The next characteristic is one that is familiar to almost everyone: General Electric is a Company with outstanding technical skills and facilities.

From the time of Edison, this has been a technical Company which has made a business of science and invention. A few other companies had early laboratories devoted to product development and working out manufacturing processes, but in 1900 General Electric established, under Dr. Willis Whitney, the General Electric Research Laboratory —the first industrial laboratory devoted to basic scientific research into the mysteries of nature.

Today, General Electric employs 18,000 technical graduates: 15,300 engineers and 2,700 scientists. To put these figures into perspective: in 1900, industry employed one engineer for every 250 employees. In 1952, the figure had risen to one engineer for every 60 employees. In General Electric, one out of every 13 employees is a scientist or engineer.*

This organization of technical skills is unique in the world. To fill in the description, you must realize that these 18,000 scientists and engineers are provided with superb facilities. These days anybody who has a Bunsen burner in the back room claims he has a research laboratory; but in terms of major installations, General Electric has 42 full-scale laboratories, plus great quantities of laboratory equipment, computers, and instruments in many other locations. Since the last world war, the Company has expended $175 million in research and development laboratories. It has also invested more than a billion dollars in the most modern plant and equipment to assure manufacturing leadership as well as research and engineering leadership.

TAKING LONG-TERM RISKS

Having these technical skills and facilities, General Electric also has the capacity—and the inclination—to take large, long-term risks in introducing

---

* Because of the large number of engineering and other functional skills required in General Electric's operations, payments to employees are about 41% of the Company's total costs.

new products, new businesses, and ultimately new industries. This risk-taking characteristic is based on two important factors.

First, the Company has had extensive experience in managing innovation. While each innovation is an adventure, we are developing patterns of managing and of action which enable us to reduce the risk, or at least calculate it better, and also to reduce the time involved in bringing new products and systems to market profitably.

The second factor in risk-taking is the Company's financial flow, which arises from its diversity and scale of operation in the economy's competitive market places. The relative stability of General Electric's total sales volume and profit makes it possible to invest in the development of products and markets which may be years in reaching a state of profitability.

It is important to recognize the role of profits in innovation. Some economists have come up with the interesting theory that profits are essentially wages for innovation. It is equally true that innovations subsist on profits, eating them up voraciously, and when one considers the amount of profit that is used in the development of, say, man-made diamonds, or silicone insulating resins, or transistors, or atomic-power reactors, it is perfectly plain why steady profits are so necessary for a company that hopes to bring new and better products and systems to the American people.

I have read of legislators who want to impose extra taxes on the profits of large corporations, to "equalize" their capacity to innovate—that is, to reduce it to the level of companies that cannot or will not take the long-term risks involved in bringing new industries to birth. This is questionable economics. Where would the truly big, difficult, long-term risks be undertaken? Can we afford to tax innovation—which means the innovation of new jobs, new purchasing power, new standards of living, and, indeed, of new small supply and retailing companies themselves—can we afford to tax basic research and innovation out of existence? Obviously, this would not be in the public interest.

"GROWING FROM WITHIN"

The emphasis on technical innovation and risk brings us logically to the next characteristic of the Company: General Electric "grows from within." The Company is expanding not by merger or purchase of other companies, but by developing new products and markets, and hence new businesses.

Experience has taught General Electric people to see each product as a type of organism, with a life cycle of its own. There is the laborious process of bringing a new product to birth, from its abstract beginnings in scientific thought or in some salesman's perception of a customer need. Then the expensive period when this new product, like a child, is not fully developed and not able to support itself. As the Company is able to develop a market—and keep the product designed for the market—the product enters a growth period, when other companies are all too happy to join in the process of competing for a share of the new market. As the product becomes established, the Company must keep renewing it with fresh innovations and features. And finally, some totally new approach makes the product obsolete and it must be retired from the line while new products are brought on the market.

Thus, the Company is in the business of both innovation and obsolescence. We are attempting always to make non-electrical ways of doing things obsolete, and even to make our own products and processes obsolete with new ones.

Interesting examples of new products which are now taking a considerable investment, but which will—we hope—ultimately develop into important new businesses, are the Weathertron and the gas turbine.

The Weathertron is a heat pump which heats and air conditions your home through winter and summer with no fuel supply except electricity. Once the market for this product is fully established, the Company will benefit not only from the sale of Weathertrons but also from the sale of power generation, transmission, and distribution equipment which results from the increased demand for electric power.

The gas turbine is another new product—the off-shoot of our steam turbine and jet engine technology. General Electric has risked literally tens of millions in developing this product and the market for it, but it is already serving in many useful applications: in power stations, in gas pipeline pumping, in locomotives, and in ship propulsion.

Both these products thus are developing into important new industries, with lively competition from other concerns once the market is established, and with new employment opportunities for thousands of our fellow citizens. It is by choice and by design that the Company's motto reads, "Progress Is Our Most Important Product."

DIVERSIFICATION

As a natural result of being in the electrical business, with a long tradition of research and innovation, General Electric may well be the most diversified Company in the world. Surprisingly, it is almost impossible to say how many different products the Company manufactures because it is impossible to get agreement on just what a "product" is. For example, consider the circular fluorescent lamp and the straight fluorescent lamp. Are they two products, or one product? Is a pink fluorescent a different product from a yellow-tinged one?

One brave soul ventured the estimate that General Electric manufactures 200,000 separate products, and it is a statistical fact that the Company lists more than 3 million catalog numbers to differentiate various sizes, shapes, and ratings. As far as bookkeeping is concerned, separate operating records are kept today on about 350 lines of products, and there are nearly 100 product-manufacturing operating departments,* as well as numerous distributing and selling departments.

* On the average, each one of the departments is equivalent to a $30 to $40 million company.

Yet, in spite of the tremendous variety, these are not miscellaneous or unrelated products. All these products have their base in the fundamental business of creating and serving the market for equipment to make, transmit, distribute, and use electric power.

What has happened is that, although the Company started with the basic technology of electrical engineering, the technologies diversified as its engineers ran into new technical barriers. For example, our designs very early encountered technical limits in insulating materials. The Company needed insulating capacities that were not commercially available, and was thus obliged to enter into chemical research in order to develop its own special materials. Likewise, many of the Company's products from lamps to turbines have from the beginning been limited primarily by the kinds of metals that have been available. So, in order to produce more efficient turbines and to provide the customer with a lamp that will give more light for his money, General Electric has engaged in metallurgical research and has become a producer of special metals.

Thus, as we overcome new scientific and technical barriers, we see a merging of old technologies, the rise of new technologies, and the growth of fresh businesses which have an actual, but not always obvious, basis in the primary technology of producing and utilizing electric power.

This flow of scientific discoveries and new business opportunities has given General Electric a logical interest in some of the promising new fields of the future: industrial electronics and automation; air conditioning and the heat pump; gas turbines; rockets and guided missiles; atomic energy; the high-strength, heat-resistant metals, ceramics, and chemicals; and the ever new and challenging field of electrical appliances and equipment.

As of today, the Company's sales volume consists of approximately 35% consumer products, 25% user products, for business and industry, 20% highly engineered defense, electronics, and atomic products, and 20% components and materials chiefly for other manufacturers. This diversity brings the Company into active, direct competition with about 600 other principal companies. In some lines we have achieved competitive leadership and are working hard to deserve to maintain or improve that volume. In other lines, frankly, some of our competitors are pleasing more people than we are. General Electric is out to earn customer acceptance and satisfaction in every product line it produces, by giving the customer the product values and service that will win his support in the market place.

SIZE

The tenth distinctive characteristic of General Electric is its size. It is big. General Electric has, in the United States, 138 plants in 107 cities in 28 states. In addition, the Company operates a number of atomic energy installations for the government and has sales or production facilities in many foreign countries.

In 1955, the Company's sales volume amounted to $3,095,000,000, and net earnings after taxes were $201,000,000. The Company's objective is to double its dollar sales volume by 1963 and improve its rate of earnings.

LONG-RANGE VIEWPOINT

The final characteristic I should like to call to your attention is General Electric's long-range point of view. This is becoming increasingly characteristic of all business in this country, and presents a great new stabilizing factor in the economy. It is a natural point of view in the innovation business, where we look on products over their probable life span, and see our role as performing a continuous innovation function.

Because of General Electric's size and diversity, its widespread popular ownership, and its customer-relationship with practically every family in the United States, the Company's fortunes are intricately related to the factors shaping the economy and society. Management is therefore obliged to anticipate long-range changes and compute their effect on the business.

This is all in the public interest. It assures that the corporation will not take an expedient, short-term, irresponsible attitude toward the public that it serves. We are concerned not only with today's customers, but with their children, and their children's children, whom we hope to number among the Company's customers in the future.

This completes my description of the General Electric Company. If it has been over-long, let me apologize, but it is a difficult assignment to describe accurately in any case, and I suppose my affection for the Company has led me into a description of features which would not be of vital interest to everyone, even students of management.

Now, by way of introduction to the decentralization philosophy which is giving this Company new vitality and effectiveness, let me cite some of the challenges that faced General Electric as it entered the postwar era.

CHALLENGES OF THE POSTWAR ERA

The Company faced the same external challenges as the rest of business, although perhaps they have a special significance for large corporations. Among the most important of these were four troublesome conditions that still stand as active and potential roadblocks to economic and social progress. They are: (1) excessively high taxes which are structured to penalize success and initiative; (2) growing, unchecked union power which too often tends to seek its own ends, regardless of the consequences for the great majority of the people; (3) a fantastically growing federal government, highly centralized, tending to exert more and more control over the nation's economic life; and (4) the latent suspicion of "big business," a tempting target for demagogues who are hunting for votes regardless of the economic and social consequences.

For purposes of these lectures, we are even more concerned with the challenges and opportunities that were internal to the Company, arising from its structure, scale, and individual characteristics. Here are some of the questions that were being asked by management, as we entered the postwar era:

How can a Company of such size and diversity be made more manageable? In fact, how can it be kept from becoming unmanageable?

How can the Company be structured for continuous and rapid growth, to serve the country's expanding and competitive markets?

How can the Company be kept profitable? This question becomes increasingly difficult to answer in a period of spiraling taxes and labor costs, and rapid obsolescence of products and facilities.

How can leaders be developed for the bigger, more complex Company of tomorrow?

How can General Electric remain fully competitive with at least 600 active and growing competitors in many different fields?

How can we assure that the Company's large size will continue to be an advantage rather than a disadvantage to everyone concerned?

How can the Company keep abreast of new knowledge in so many fields, and put it to work for customers—faster and more profitably than competitors?

How can we assure that General Electric will contribute its fair share to the sum of human knowledge?

How can management plan ahead accurately? How can the corporation be kept from drifting into complacency and irresponsibility?

How can General Electric continue to win the understanding, approval, and support of all the groups that have an interest in its operations?

In summary, what must be done to see that this great corporation will be managed in the balanced best interests of all and will meet the ethical as well as the material expectations of our fellow citizens?

The Company's response to these challenges is summed up in the word "decentralization." This, the philosophy and practice of decentralization in General Electric, will be the subject of the next lecture.

DECENTRALIZATION:
A MANAGERIAL
PHILOSOPHY

Every company should be managed in accordance with some workable, ethically responsible philosophy of management. That is, the managers of the company should be in general agreement on a set of underlying principles that will guide their work in providing leadership for the company.

For some companies, the set of principles that guide the managers may be tacitly understood, without ever being presented systematically. They may be part of the company's tradition or may even reflect the personal philosophy of the chief executive.

While General Electric's present philosophy of management has had a long evolution in Company tradition and reflects the personalities of its great leaders in years gone by, considerable effort has been devoted in the past ten years to "thinking through" and presenting this managerial philosophy in a systematic way.

In this lecture, I should like to discuss the results of these studies: the philosophy of decentralization, and how it has been applied by General Electric in building an organization structure to meet the challenges of an expanding economy.

At the very outset, let me make clear that I am not selling our particular approach to organizing and managing as a solution for the problems of other companies. If I have any thesis, it is that each company should study, for itself, the particular conditions that will determine its future, and out of such detailed study should evolve a philosophy and structure that is fully appropriate for an individual company. The patterns of organization with which I shall deal are General Electric's solutions to General Electric's problems, and may or may not be applicable elsewhere.

REVIEWING THE CHARACTERISTICS OF GENERAL ELECTRIC

The General Electric Company faces certain opportunities and challenges that are natural results of its own particular characteristics. At the risk of being repetitious, let me summarize these characteristics here:

1. General Electric is the leading manufacturer in the electrical industry, which is probably the most sustained and dynamic growth industry of the twentieth century.

2. General Electric is owned by 358,000 share owners, one of the most widely owned companies in the world. Approximately one half of the Company's quarter million employees are now or are becoming share owners in the Company.

3. General Electric is managed by professional managers, who are not the owners of the business but employees hired by the share owners through their elected directors and the Company Officers, to manage their business in the balanced best interests of all concerned. Seventeen of the nineteen directors are non-officers, or "outside" directors.

4. The Company has a long tradition of public responsibility and integrity, as demonstrated by its participation in national, community, and educational affairs, and its services in the national defense.

5. General Electric is a customer-focused Company. Through this emphasis on serving the customer, it has also provided great benefits for share

owners, employees, suppliers, retailers, and others who share in the work of serving these customers.

6. This is a Company with outstanding technical skills and facilities, where one out of every thirteen employees is a scientist or engineer.

7. General Electric has the capacity—and the inclination—to take large, long-term risks in introducing new products, new businesses, and ultimately new industries.

8. General Electric grows from within. It is expanding not by merger or purchase of other companies, but by developing new products and markets —and hence new businesses.

9. General Electric is one of the most diversified companies in the world, with some 350 distinct product lines and about 3 million catalog items. These products have an original basis in the technologies involved in producing equipment to generate, transmit, distribute, and utilize electric power.

10. General Electric is a large company that has grown in service to the nation and the world. Its sales volume in 1955 was more than $3 billion, and its net earnings were $201 million. It provides rewarding opportunities for 252,000 employees in the United States and 29,000 employees in foreign lands, for 40,000 suppliers, and for 400,000 dis-

tributive-type businesses which derive all or part of their income from selling and servicing General Electric products.

11. General Electric needs to be managed with a long-range point of view, which is natural for a company in the business of innovation.

Out of these eleven characteristics of the General Electric Company arise its particular challenges and opportunities, and the particular forms of management and organization that are practiced in the Company.

EXPLOSIVE GROWTH RAISES
ORGANIZATIONAL QUESTIONS

Up until 1939, the Company was able to operate efficiently under a highly centralized form of management. During World War II, however, General Electric began a period of almost explosive growth which caused its managers to question whether it might not be necessary to evolve new techniques of organizing and managing the Company.

From 1920 to 1939, the Company's sales volume had risen slowly from $200 million to $342 million a year. By 1943, under the pressure of war production, it rose suddenly to $1,370,000,000 a year—over a four-fold increase in four years. Postwar experience and forecasts indicated that this was only the beginning of an opportunity for continuing, rapid growth in serving the nation's demands for electrical and related products. The Company produced over $3 billion worth of goods and services last year; and if we do the job we should do of satisfying customers, this figure may well rise—as the Company has publicly stated many times—to $6 billion early in the 1960's.

It is obvious that a Company with such growth characteristics, and operating on such a scale, requires a different managerial approach than the Company of the 1920's and '30's. This was, of course, recognized by Gerard Swope, who served as president during those decades when the foundations for future growth were carefully laid, and by Charles Wilson, the Company's president during the hectic, war-torn '40's. Under their leadership, I was asked to study the new problems of organizing and managing such a rapidly growing enterprise.

From the beginning of the study, it was apparent that the Company was going to require increasingly better planning, greater flexibility, and faster, more informed decisions than was possible under the highly centralized organization structure, which was suited for earlier and different conditions. Unless we could put the responsibility and authority for decision making closer in each case to the scene of the problem, where complete understanding and prompt action are possible, the Company would not be able to compete with the hundreds of nimble competitors who were, as they say, able to turn on a dime.

In addition, General Electric faced the need to develop capable leaders for the future; the need for more friendly and cooperative relationships between managers and other employees; the need to stay ahead of competition in serving the customers; and the very human need to make the work of a manager at all echelons of the organization more manageable. The work had to be made more manageable so that it could be understood and carried out by people of normally available energy and intelligence, thus leaving no requirement for the so-called indispensable man.

THE SOLUTION: DECENTRALIZATION

To these and many other challenges which were described in my previous lecture, the philosphy of decentralization seemed to provide useful solutions.

Now, decentralization has different meanings for

different people. The decision to decentralize General Electric did not mean that it was decided to "break up the Company" into smaller pieces. This would be self-defeating, because it would lose to the public and to the Company those advantages that are the distinctive contribution of large enterprises: the ability to serve as a source of major innovations in the nation's economic life, creating new products, new industries, new employment, and new outlets for smaller businesses; the ability to energize the flow of mass production and mass distribution; and the ability to provide a broad range of advanced technical capacity in order to produce the more complex products and systems of our times.

In General Electric, decentralization is a way of preserving and enhancing these contributions of the large enterprise, and at the same time achieving the flexibility and the "human touch" that are popularly associated with—though not always attained by—small organizations.

Under this concept, we have undertaken decentralization not only according to products, geography, and functional types of work. The most important aspect of the Company's philosophy is thorough decentralization of the responsibility and authority for making business decisions.

47

Here is the underlying logic. The share owners, through their Board of Directors, delegate to the President responsibility for the conduct of the whole business. The responsibility carries with it all the authority required to get the work done, except such authorities as are specifically withheld by the Board and the share owners. The total responsibility also carries with it full accountability for results. General Electric may be unique in that the Board of Directors has issued a position guide for the President, stating in detail his responsibility, authority, and accountability.

Now, the President is of course unable to do all the work himself, and so he delegates the responsibility for portions of the total work through organization channels to individuals who have the talents and knowledge required to do it. This is done by planning and building the work of the Company into an organization structure which consists of all the necessary positions and components required to do all the work in the most effective and efficient manner.

Each employee thus takes on responsibility for some part of the over-all Company work. Along with this responsibility, each position naturally carries with it full accountability for measured results, and all the necessary authority required for the position except those authorities that are specifically stated as withheld. Therefore each employee of the Company has, in his position, full responsibility, authority, and accountability for a certain defined body of work and teamwork. Through teamwork he recognizes his relationships to the other employees who perform a share of the total work of the Company.

With this philosophy, General Electric achieves a community of purpose between leaders and their associates, and is able to attain that voluntary integration which is the hallmark of a free and decentralized enterprise.

In such compressed statement, this management philosophy may sound somewhat obscure, but its practical result is to put the responsibility for making business decisions not with a few top executives, but with the individual managerial and functional employees who have the most immediately applicable information required to make sound decisions and take prompt action. When such responsibility—along with commensurate authority and accountability—has been delegated according to a carefully planned organization of work, then each individual in the Company has a challenging and dignified position which will bring out his full resources and enthusiastic cooperation.

TEN GUIDING PRINCIPLES

Since philosophy is, by definition, a system of first principles, I should like to list for you ten principles which express General Electric's philosophy of decentralization.

1. Decentralization places authority to make decisions at points as near as possible to where actions take place.

2. Decentralization is likely to get best over-all results by getting greatest and most directly applicable knowledge and most timely understanding actually into play on the greatest number of decisions.

3. Decentralization will work if real authority is delegated; and not if details then have to be reported, or, worse yet, if they have to be "checked" first.

4. Decentralization requires confidence that associates in decentralized positions will have the capacity to make sound decisions in the majority of cases; and such confidence starts at the executive level. Unless the President and all the other Officers have a deep personal conviction and an active desire

to decentralize full decision-making responsibility and authority, actual decentralization will never take place. The Officers must set an example in the art of full delegation.

5. Decentralization requires understanding that the main role of staff or services is the rendering of assistance and advice to line operators through a relatively few experienced people, so that those making decisions can themselves make them correctly.

6. Decentralization requires realization that the natural aggregate of many individually sound decisions will be better for the business and for the public than centrally planned and controlled decisions.

7. Decentralization rests on the need to have general business objectives, organization structure, relationships, policies, and measurements known, understood, and followed; but realizing that definition of policies does not necessarily mean uniformity of methods of executing such policies in decentralized operations.

8. Decentralization can be achieved only when higher executives realize that authority genuinely delegated to lower echelons cannot, in fact, also be retained by them. We have, today, Officers and Managers who still believe in decentralization down to themselves and no further. By paying lip-service

to decentralization, but actually reviewing detailed work and decisions and continually "second-guessing" their associates, such Officers keep their organization in confusion and prevent the growth of self-reliant men.

9. Decentralization will work only if responsibility commensurate with decision-making authority is truly accepted and exercised at all levels.

10. Decentralization requires personnel policies based on measured performance, enforced standards, rewards for good performance, and removal for incapacity or poor performance.

DESIGNING ORGANIZATIONAL STRUCTURE

Now, given this philosophy, how can it be expressed in an organization structure suitable to the General Electric Company? In our experience, the following work must be done to attain a sound, flexible, and dynamic organization structure:

1. Determine the objectives, and the policies, programs, plans, and schedules that will best achieve those objectives; for the Company as a whole and in turn, for each component of the business.

2. Determine the work to be done to achieve these objectives, under such guiding policies.

3. Divide and classify or group related work into a

simple, logical, understandable, and comprehensive organization structure.

4. Assign essential work clearly and definitely to the various components and positions in the organization structure.

5. Determine the requirements and qualifications of personnel to occupy such positions.

6. Staff the organization with persons who meet these qualifications.

7. Establish methods and procedures which will help to achieve the objectives of the organization.

This is the procedure which has been followed in carrying out General Electric's current decentralization program, which had its beginnings in studies started in 1943, and went into the actual application phase in February, 1951. As you can imagine, the entire process involves a tremendous amount of self-analysis and education throughout the organization. Not only new ideas, but new attitudes need to be developed and accepted. Many former positions and organizations need to be discontinued, and many new and responsible positions and components are created. Persons may feel, under such changing circumstances, that their careers and livelihoods are threatened, so that they may be inclined to be suspicious, or at least over-cautious, until the new philosophy has been thoroughly assimilated, refined, and established. Timing is of the utmost importance, and I personally felt in 1951 that five years would be required to evolve the new structure and have it implemented with understanding and enthusiasm. The program appears to be just about on schedule.

Through all these difficult conditions, the General Electric men and women have performed with admirable wisdom and maturity, maintaining the momentum of progress in serving their customers while absorbing this latest phase in the Company's evolution. The work of organization is never done, and the structure has to be continuously adapted to new and anticipated conditions. Nevertheless, it is safe to say that the new type of decentralized organization structure has been substantially established and manned, with outstanding personnel, products, and facilities to make it effective. The results, in terms of better values for customers and better earnings for share owners and employees, are reflected in the Company's statement for the first quarter of 1956, which shows an increase of 14% in sales and 30% in orders, over the first quarter of 1955.

GENERAL ELECTRIC'S OBJECTIVES

I indicated that the first step in organization is to sharpen up the objectives of the Company as a whole, to provide a framework for the objectives of each organization component and each position in the Company.

These Company objectives have been subjected to deep study, and are still undergoing review by managers throughout the organization. At present, they are ten in number and broad in character, and they are reflected in the Company's organization structure. Briefly summarized, General Electric's objectives are as follows: *

1. To carry on a diversified, growing, and profitable worldwide manufacturing business in electrical apparatus, appliances, and supplies, and in related materials, products, systems, and services for industry, commerce, agriculture, government, the community, and the home.

2. To lead in research in all fields of science and all areas of work relating to the business in order to assure a constant flow of new knowledge that will

* The objectives of the Company are stated in full in the Appendix.

make real the Company theme, "Progress Is Our Most Important Product."

3. To operate each decentralized business venture to achieve its own customer acceptance and profitable results, by taking the appropriate business risks.

4. To design, make, and market all Company products and services with good quality and with inherent customer value, at fair, competitive prices.

5. To build public confidence and friendly feeling for products and services bearing the Company's name and brands.

6. To provide good jobs, wages, working conditions, work satisfactions, stability of employment, and opportunities for advancement for employees, in return for their loyalty, initiative, skill, care, effort, attendance, and teamwork.

7. To manage the human and material resources of the enterprise for continuity and flow of progress, growth, profit, and public service in accordance with the principles of decentralization, sound organization structure, and professional management.

8. To attract and retain investor capital through attractive returns as a continuing incentive for wide investor participation and support.

9. To cooperate with suppliers, distributors, re-

tailers, contractors, and others who facilitate the production, distribution, installation, and servicing of Company products and systems.

10. To meet the Company's social, civic, and economic responsibilities with imagination and with voluntary action which will merit the understanding and support of all concerned among the public.

To the casual reader or listener, these broad objectives may sound vague and obvious, but thoughtful study will reveal that each of them represents a number of deliberate and important managerial decisions. They provide a direct expression of the Company's ethical standards, its managerial philosophy, and its continuing purposes—in a form which makes them understandable and acceptable, after study, to every member of the organization.

GENERAL ELECTRIC'S ORGANIZATION STRUCTURE

In order to achieve these objectives on a continuing and profitable basis, an improved organization structure was devised in accordance with the principles of decentralization. This structure and the reasons for it are outlined in considerable detail in a paper I presented before the American Management Association in June, 1952, but here we shall sketch only the main outline of the structure.

The organization of General Electric is essentially a three-part structure which carefully distinguishes between Operating work, Services work, and Executive work.

THE OPERATING COMPONENTS

First let us consider the Operating work. Today, General Electric's products are engineered, manufactured, and marketed by nearly a hundred decentralized Operating Departments, each of them bearing full operating responsibility and authority for the Company's success and profitability in a particular product or service field. The special skills and knowledge required for each operating business are thus brought to bear by a local business managerial team which can concentrate on the opportunities of a specific product or marketing area. Through these integrated managerial teams, each with a specific profit-and-loss responsibility for the operation of a defined business, we achieve the flexibility, drive, and the "human touch" that comes from direct participation in the daily problems of a business.

To demonstrate that the responsibility, authority, and accountability of these Operating Departments is real, not window dressing, consider their pricing authority. The price of a product can be raised or lowered by the managers of the Department producing it, with only voluntary responsibility on their part to give sensible consideration to the impact of such price changes on other Company products. In one area of General Electric products, the major appliances such as refrigerators, ranges, and home laundry equipment, there are two Divisions competing directly with each other. The Hotpoint Division in Chicago and the Major Appliance and Television Receiver Division in Louisville have different facilities, different product designs, different distribution, and different prices. They compete at the market place very aggressively, and, incidentally, very profitably. Other Departments compete with each other by presenting different types of products that perform essentially the same function. For example, there is the competition between electronic tubes and transistors, or between room air conditioners and central air conditioning.

As further evidence of the freedom provided by decentralization to the Operating Departments, consider the fact that the operating budget of the General Electric Company is not a document prepared by the Executive Offices in New York. It is an addition of the budgets prepared by the Operating Department General Managers, with the concurrence of the Division General Managers and Group Executives. These budgets include planned sales volume, product development plans, expenditures for plant and equipment, market targets, turnover of investment, net earnings, projected organization structure, and other related items.

In the days when the Company had a centralized organization, it was the custom for Operating components to submit budgets which were promptly blue-penciled, modified, expanded or contracted, and "second-guessed" by the headquarters Executives. As a result, Operating people did not usually take their budgeting too seriously.

Now they are taking it seriously because they know they will be measured on their ability to achieve the budgeted results which they, themselves, have established as proper goals for their organizations.

We are frequently asked how these Operating Departments can do accurate forecasting and budgeting, and how the Executives can delegate this difficult function to persons less broadly experienced than themselves. The Operating Departments can do better forecasting and budgeting because they are intimately informed as to the conditions which prevail and will prevail in their line of business.

Since they are better informed, they are authorized to make whatever prudent commitments they should on materials, and we have recently increased the approval authority of the Operating Department General Managers over capital expenditures so that they can, by their own decision, make commitments up to $500,000.*

In such a diversified company as General Electric, it is impossible for the Executives in New York to have detailed knowledge of such a variety of businesses and markets. Executives can help by supplying some general aiming areas for the Company as a whole, and information as to the probable general trends of business. But this information is to be factored in, and not to dominate the budgeting of the Operating Departments, nor does it do so.

The fact is that the Operating Departments are now doing better budgeting than was done by head-

---

* I believe that too much of a fetish has been made in the past of capital expenditures. A manager can lose a lot more money on inventory, foolish pricing policy, careless personnel staffing, or poor production scheduling. Let me illustrate. In General Electric, capital expenditures in 1955 amounted to $153 millions, but we bought $1,400 millions of materials and had a payroll of $1,200 millions.

quarters in years gone by. Last year the Company as a whole was within 1% of its budgeted sales results, although some individual Departments were off by substantially greater percentages one way or another.

The Operating Departments are now making plans and budgets which are firm commitments for five years and estimates for ten years. This is not on the Soviet model of the so-called "Five Year Plan" which regards each plan as a separate batch of work, to be succeeded by the next plan. Instead, a General Electric operating plan is a continuous and dynamic structure based on a rolling forecast, always ten years ahead of current operations. Frequent reviews and annual adjustments keep the plans realistically attuned to new conditions and competitive developments. Thus each is a dynamic business plan, not a rigid strait-jacket of the "planned economy" type.

It is important to emphasize the voluntary nature of a position in General Electric. For every position in the Company, including these Operating General Managers, a man has the personal right to accept or refuse the position—along with accountability for the results expected, and the risks involved in accepting such responsibilities. If for personal or other reasons he decides not to accept a particular position, there is no prejudice against him. He will receive other offers for which he is qualified as such positions become available. Voluntary and whole-hearted acceptance is of course a necessary condition if a man is to be held accountable for results in risk-taking ventures.

At the present time the Company has nearly 100 manufacturing Operating Departments, plus a number of sales and service business departments. For purposes of management, these departments are grouped into 21 Operating Divisions. Each division might be described as a family of businesses; for example, the Turbine Division consists of the Gas Turbine Department, the Large Steam Turbine-Generator Department, the Medium Steam Turbine, Generator, and Gear Department, the Small Turbine Department, and the Foundry Department.

After he has proven his capacity to be an Officer, the General Manager of a Division is usually elected a Vice President of the Company. Most of the Division General Manager's time is devoted to long-range planning for the Division as a part of the overall Company, while operating responsibilities for the specific businesses are clearly delegated to the Department General Managers.

To assure that the Operating Departments and their customers will receive the full benefit of the Company's broad resources in knowledge and risk-taking capacity, two other types of work are provided for in the Company's over-all organization structure: Services work and Executive work.

THE SERVICES

The functional services are components at the corporate level, staffed with the Company's most experienced personnel in the major business functions: accounting, engineering, legal and corporate, management consultation, manufacturing, marketing, public and employee relations, treasury, and research. It is important to note that, in contrast with the powerful Operating authority wielded by headquarters functional Executives under the earlier centralized structure, these Services people have no authority whatsoever over the Operating Departments and Divisions, except the authority of knowledge. They have, instead, two Company-wide responsibilities: to do research, teaching, and long-range guidance in personnel development in their functional field; and to do such functional operating work for the Company as a whole as can best be done at the corporate level.

First, let us consider the research and teaching—what we call "Services functional work." In each business function, such as accounting or marketing, General Electric is trying to apply the same principles of fundamental research and creative study that have long kept it ahead in the area of science and technology. The Services have been deliberately freed of Operating responsibility so that they can think ahead, developing through research the most advanced knowledge, principles, and techniques in their functional field, as well as keeping abreast of current knowledge developed elsewhere.

Services also have the responsibility to convert this new knowledge into usable forms and patterns, and to make it available through advice and teaching, to the Operating Departments and Divisions. Services also help to formulate Company policies appropriate to their function, and maintain a "clearinghouse" of current practices and standards within the Company to help facilitate a free flow of functional knowledge across the entire organization.

Of course, communications should never bog down in channels. If a Section Manager in steam turbine engineering at Schenectady, for example, wants some information pertaining to the engineering of aircraft gas turbines in another section, in

Evendale, he does not have to go all the way up through channels to a Group Executive and down the other channel. He is expected to get the information straight across the Company just by picking up the telephone and talking to the fellow in Evendale who has the information.

The duties of Services also include long-range personnel development planning, to assure a continuing supply of outstanding people with the required changing functional skills.

Thus the emphasis in Service functional work is on the future: anticipating future opportunities and future problems, so that when they arrive General Electric will have the personnel and knowledge ready to meet them unsurprised.

The other important duty of the Services is to perform such operating work as can best be done at the corporate level, for the Company as a whole.

This includes, for example, the work of Treasury Services in handling corporate financing and investment activities on an efficient basis. There would be great confusion if the 21 Operating Divisions or 100 Operating Departments were to deal with the banks entirely separately. It should be remembered, however, that the authority to deny the use of capital from the Company's treasury to Operating General Managers who wish prudently to invest is not part of the Treasurer's responsibilities.

Another example of Operating work in the Services is the conduct of public relations programs such as institutional advertising and television, preparation of the annual report, and similar informational activities that deal with the Company as a whole. It is important that Services perform such corporate operating work with great distinction, to serve as a high standard for functional work throughout the Company.

THE EXECUTIVES

Leadership and long-range planning for the Company as a whole constitute the Executive classification of work in the Company structure. To understand this Executive aspect of the General Electric organization, it is important to understand two unusual organizational devices: The President's Office and the Executive Office.

The President's Office is a group of Executives who share the work of the President. In addition to the President, it includes the Chairman of the Board, and five Executive Vice Presidents. The Chairman of the Board, in addition to the duties assigned him directly by the Board, represents the

President in such areas as financial affairs, public and governmental liaison, and international matters, and each of the Executive Vice Presidents represents the President in relationships with a specific group of Operating Divisions. This unique organizational device was created in recognition of the fact that no one man would have the time and knowledge required to provide effective Executive leadership for the variety of businesses in a Company as large and as diversified as General Electric. Thus each Executive Vice President serves as the President in a defined Operating area, without in any sense relieving the President of the ultimate responsibility placed upon him by the Board of Directors for the success of the enterprise as a whole.

The Executive Vice Presidents, in General Electric, are true Executives. That is, they have been freed of Operating responsibility and administrative details so that they can devote their time to long-range planning, appraisal of current performance, bringing divisional objectives and plans into a working pattern with over-all Company needs, and making sure of the needed continuity of competent managerial and other personnel in the decentralized businesses.

These seven members of the President's Office, together with the nine Company Officers in charge of the Services, form what is known as the Executive Office. These Senior Officers deliberately set aside about 20% of their time to serve, not as Executives for their particular area of Operations or Services, but as a well-balanced group of general Executives who advise the President on matters that concern all functions and all operations—in other words, the Company as a whole. In this way the Executive Office provides a melding of extensive business judgment and advanced functional knowledge to help the President plan the Company's management, growth, and course ten or more years ahead.

There you have the organizational structure of the General Electric Company: a three-part structure consisting of the Executives, who provide leadership and long-range planning for the Company as a whole; the Services, which provide leadership and advanced research in each functional field; and the Operating components, which have decentralized responsibility for the success, growth, and competitive profitability of the Company's diverse Operating businesses.

A significant feature of this organization is that it

has no place for assistants, "assistants-to," or "administrative assistants." It is our firm belief that such titles or positions create confusion as to responsibility, authority, and accountability, and tend to retard the growth of men and the Company. If a position is too big for one person and appears to require assistants, then the work should be divided up and reorganized into as many positions as are required to do the work efficiently. Each position in the Company should be able to "stand on its own," with a specifically defined area of responsibility, authority, and accountability.

Likewise, General Electric structure has no place for committees as decision-making bodies. It is my feeling that a committee moves at the speed of its least informed member, and too often is used as a way of sharing irresponsibility. Before decentralization, an official tried to get on a great number of committees. He would lead a very calm, safe, orderly life. Not much would happen, but nothing would ever happen to him.

Today, a committee may be helpful as an advisory group, and indeed the Executive Office of the General Electric Company meets twice monthly as an Advisory Council for the President. In any such arrangement, however, it must be made abundantly clear that the authority for any particular decision lies with the responsible individual, even if he makes it while sitting with the other Council members.

Such a deliberate avoidance of assistants and decision-making committees is directly in keeping with the decentralization philosophy, which requires full delegation of responsibility, authority, and accountability to the person who is best qualified to make the decisions for a certain area of work.

CHALLENGES OF DECENTRALIZATION

Bringing this decentralized organization structure to full effectiveness poses a number of immediate challenges to every member of the organization, and particularly to the managers. These include:

The development of men.

Leadership by persuasion rather than command.

The achievement of teamwork, integration, and balance.

The measurement of results.

Proper use of all types of compensation.

Criteria for determining the scope of a business at Department and Division levels, and for the Company as a whole.

We can touch on only a few of these challenging topics, but in the next lecture I will take up in greater detail these and other frontier areas for professional managers.

DEVELOPMENT OF MEN

First, consider the development of men. Our studies indicate that this challenge will be met by applying four concepts:

The first concept is self-development. The Company has a policy of equal opportunity for every employee to develop and advance just as far and as rapidly as he can. It is part of each manager's work to challenge and guide those who report to him, in their self-development planning. But the initiative, the spark, must be provided by the man himself.

The second concept is "climate for growth." The Company's research into the processes of manpower development indicates that the growth—or lack of growth—of strong leaders and self-reliant individuals depends a great deal on what we call "managerial climate." This "tone" or "atmosphere" in an organization can be subjected to analysis and a certain degree of measurement. Furthermore, the manager and the individuals in the component can do specific things to improve the climate, so that men will develop faster and work will be done more effectively and enthusiastically.

The third concept is manpower planning. This is the manager's work. He needs to plan ahead specifically for his future requirements and then begin to develop people who will be qualified for future openings in his own component and throughout the Company.

The fourth concept for manpower development is increased education. The complexities of modern business demand ever higher levels of education among employees. Industry is therefore obliged to step up its own adult educational activities, and to utilize more fully the resources of the nation's educational institutions. In General Electric, one out of eight General Electric employees at all levels of the organization takes advantage of Company-conducted courses, in an average year. The cost of this educational and training activity in General Electric is on the order of $35 to $40 million a year.

Such activities range all the way from factory courses to retrain employees for changes in assignments, to advanced educational courses for professional employees in every function, including the function of management. By the end of the year 1956, about 4,000 General Electric men will be taking the Professional Business Management Course in decentralized components across the country.

Within three years it is expected that 25,000 employees will have completed this course of study.

Just this year, General Electric completed construction and began operation of a Management Research and Development Institute at Crotonville, New York. In addition to training leaders for the Professional Business Management Course, the Institute conducts an Advanced Management Course for classes of 80 carefully selected employees who spend 13 weeks at the Institute, away from their regular duties. The Institute is thus serving as a focal point for a major Company-wide effort in manager education.

LEADING BY PERSUASION

Another major challenge posed by the decentralization philosophy is the challenge to lead by persuasion rather than command. This is inherent in the very idea of decentralization. I do not think that I exaggerate when I say that about 20% of the time of the Officers is spent talking to employees at all levels, exploring and answering questions to arrive at a common understanding of what the Company is and what it is trying to do.

A centralized organization implies control from a central point, with close supervision and issuance of orders and mandatory courses of action, so that the centralized control can be effective. Decentralization, on the other hand, implies freedom for individuals everywhere in the organization to act on the basis of their own knowledge of the particular conditions that apply to the particular problem at hand. This does not mean that a decentralized organization should be loose-jointed or uncoordinated. On the contrary, even more effective and flexible integration can be achieved through the formulation and communication of common objectives and policies, and common means for measurement, so that the man in the decentralized components of the organization will voluntarily and responsibly make sound decisions in the interests of the entire enterprise.

In this situation, the manager's work is to lead others by drawing out their ideas, their special knowledge, and their efforts. Since self-discipline rather than boss-discipline is the hallmark of a decentralized organization, the manager resorts to command only in emergencies where he must admit temporary failure to make the situation and the necessary course of action self-evident. To the degree that the contributions of every individual are made voluntarily and are self-disciplined, the manager is leading by persuasion rather than command.

INTEGRATION, TEAMWORK, AND BALANCE

A third challenge of decentralization is the challenge of integration, teamwork, and balance. There is no question but that decentralization can set up powerful centrifugal forces that could pull a company apart. We have had to discourage managers from pre-empting, through squatters' rights, everything they could see. They had been suppressed by strong hands, and the power and authority given to them under decentralization was raw meat. Maybe they were "overtrained" because they sometimes became so independent that they wanted neither advice nor restrictions in the interests of the whole Company. I am greatly concerned when a man talks about "my organization," "my Division," or "my men," for all of us are just passing by.

There is a need for some practical instruments to assure that local decisions will recognize and advance the interests of the Company as a whole, rather than work at cross-purposes with the rest of the organization.

One basic instrument is the formulation and communication of clear objectives for the Company as a whole. Then each component can establish its own objectives to help attain, rather than contradict, the objectives of the whole enterprise. This is why it is important that a company's objectives be studied and understood by everyone in the organization.*

Another need is for policies which clearly express the common interests and the common purposes of all members of the enterprise. It is important that the number of policies be kept to a minimum, and my opinion is that about 50 policies should suffice to spell out the policy considerations of the General Electric Company. In most situations, the policy merely requires that conscious and orderly thought be given to the over-all business enterprise before important local decisions are made. Only in a very few fields is use made of directive policies which prescribe a mandatory course of action based on a corporate rather than a local decision.

Yet another instrument of integration is a system of common nomenclature, a common language in

* The objectives of the General Electric Company are stated in the Appendix.

describing the work classifications, and positions, and the organizational components of the Company.

However, beyond such formal means as common objectives, policies, and nomenclature, the integration of a decentralized company requires an active understanding and acceptance of the concept of deliberate and voluntary teamwork. The concepts of teamwork, integration, and balanced effort need to prevail or the company can drift inevitably toward recentralization. Hence the Company's managers, in order to preserve their freedom of decision-making, need deeply to learn the habits of voluntary teamwork in the interests of the enterprise as a whole.

A PHILOSOPHY OF FREEDOM

What I have said of decentralization as a philosophy applies with equal force to any large organization of free human beings, whether it be a government, a university, a union, or a business. Decentralization is a creative response to the challenges of our time, a way of preserving and enhancing the competitive enterprise system as it evolves into the new forms that have been so aptly named the "people's capitalism."

Decentralization: A Managerial Philosophy

The economy of the United States, and its position as a world power, make large enterprises both an irreversible fact and an actual necessity for economic and national security reasons. Any attendant perils lie not in bigness itself, but in the way the energies of large organizations are organized and managed. Centralized administration of large institutions of any kind can lead to irresponsibility, shortsightedness, inefficiency, and the abuse of power—but this need not happen under wise and self-disciplined guidance. Responsible decentralization—as a philosophy—makes it possible to provide at once the big results that come from big enterprises, with the human freedom that comes from respecting the competence and dignity of every individual in the enterprise.

General Electric's particular form of decentralization may or may not be applicable elsewhere, but it is built firmly on the chosen philosophy that recognizes the dignity and capacity of the individual human being, and recognizes his responsibility and authority for making the decisions that count. This philosophy, I deeply urge, must prevail if freedom is to survive in the world.

BREAKTHROUGH
TO THE
FUTURE

In the first two lectures, we have been concerned with the present characteristics, the present philosophy, and the present structure of the General Electric Company. From this descriptive material I hope you have found a better understanding of the Company and its approach to organization and managing, as an example of the expanding enterprise in today's economy.

However, we would not fulfill the purposes of these lectures if we did not lift our eyes to the future and try to discern those challenges and opportunities which will engage professional management, particularly of expanding enterprises, in the years ahead. This will be the object of this third and final lecture, which might be entitled "Breakthrough to the Future."

We live today in an expanding universe. Just as

mathematicians and astronomers have postulated that the universe of space and time is expanding outward in all directions, at incredible speed—so, in our time, the *human* universe of knowledge, capacity, and achievement has been expanding rapidly in all directions.

On a worldwide scale and on a national scale, one sees not merely a steady advance along a single line, such as technology, but an explosion of change and growth in almost every area of human endeavor: social, political, economic, and technological.

The professional manager in the United States finds this time of accelerating change particularly challenging because our country is at the forefront of the industrial nations. The United States is rapidly advancing toward new frontiers of economic achievement, where there is little in human experience to serve as a guide.

This rush forward has been characterized by some observers as a historic breakthrough from the economics of scarcity into the economics of abundance. In this great human adventure, the professional managers, who have done so much to create these unprecedented conditions, will have both the opportunity and the responsibility to provide creative vision and responsible leadership.

THREE FRONTIER AREAS

Looking at business and finance broadly, with emphasis on the large organizations that are the subject of study in these lectures, it would appear that the most urgent challenges to managers in the coming decade will lie in three relatively unexplored areas.

First, the area of long-range planning. In a time of radical worldwide change, when every day introduces new elements of uncertainty, forward planning may seem to be nearly impossible—an exercise in futility. Yet there never was a more urgent need for long-range planning on the part of every business, and indeed every other important element of our national life.

Second, the area of organizing, communicating, and utilizing information for decision-making. Business risks today tend increasingly to have long-term, and often irreversible effects. In the large enterprises, at least, it is no longer possible or sensible for professional managers to make sound decisions wholly by intuition and a few traditional measurements. The manager of the future must increasingly base his decisions on accurate, organized knowledge. In this area, we will explore particularly the opportunities for better communication, better measurement, and better organization of the information required to operate a business.

The third frontier area to be considered in this lecture will be the baffling area of human motivations. The manager may have a purposeful vision of the future, implied in long-range planning. He may be able to develop the patterns of order and the information systems required to achieve his plans. But they will be relatively ineffective unless he can win the wholehearted support of customers, share owners, employees, suppliers, and the public, whose understanding and actions will turn the brave dreams into reality. In this area of motivations the manager is dealing with the core challenges of the industrial society: what do people want out of life, and how can these human aspirations be realized in their daily work?

To the businessman of an earlier day, and indeed to many today, these areas of challenge might appear vague and remote from business realities. General Electric is convinced that, far from being remote, these matters of long-range planning, of organizing information for decision-making, and of human motivations are among the critical areas of the future, where organized research and self-disciplined managerial action will pay continuing dividends in the form of more profitable operations, expanding opportunities, and broader, more acceptable customer service.

LONG-RANGE PLANNING

Consider the need for long-range planning. Many business organizations in the United States today are just beginning to learn to plan five years ahead. Some are actually planning ahead for the next decade. Far fewer are seriously studying the range of possible conditions that will face their successors in the next business generation. Is this good enough for the United States?

The hallmark of leadership is the ability to anticipate the reasonably foreseeable needs of tomorrow and beyond tomorrow with at least some clarity and confidence. Yet it is all too easy to become preoccupied with the day-to-day barometers, to settle for the quick, current gain. Far too often our noses seem to be buried in the daily marketing reports, the weekly carloadings, the monthly inventories, and the charts of fiscal statistics, even though these are already history as they come to our eyes.

Anyone who has had managerial experience realizes the heavy and sometimes determining influence exercised on today's operations by the major decisions and actions which he and others took five, ten, or even twenty years ago to produce today's resources and opportunities. The principal concern of business leaders today should be: what decisions and plans need to be made now, what resources should be committed, what effort should be put forth, to be certain that the Company will be in a position to meet the challenging new conditions of the future and fulfill its opportunities?

There are at work today a number of new imperatives which give the business leader—along with the political leader, the educational leader, and others—no practical alternative except to take a long-range point of view.

First, there are the pressures of a changing population. In the coming decade, the number of consumers in the United States is expected to increase more rapidly than the number of producers. It is estimated that in 1966 the people of the United States will want about 40% more goods and services than at present—and these must apparently be produced with only 14% more workers.

The acceptable solution to this dilemma is to continue to increase productivity, chiefly by forward-looking investments in automation and other technological improvements. If this technological progress is hampered by short-sightedness on the part of businessmen, union officials, politicians, or any other element of society, the nation will tragically miss its opportunities for economic advances that will benefit everyone, and we will have a decade of ruinous shortages and resultant inflation.

The second imperative that makes long-range planning necessary is the determination of the American people that steadily rising levels of living, along with economic stability, are both desirable and achievable.

Make no mistake about it: this decision has been made by the people, and they are going to pursue it by one means or another. The remarkable increase in consumer credit, the sharp rise in insurance and pension funds, the intense political activity for the so-called "government stabilizers" in the national economy—all these are significant symptoms of a deep national commitment to a long-range view of life which envisions continuing efforts to achieve manageable stability of employment in a competitive market, and rising levels of income.

Viewed creatively, these new consumer attitudes present magnificent opportunities for all businesses, provided that business managers will make wise and far-sighted plans to meet the challenge. But if the people's aims are ignored, they will turn instead to short-sighted political and economic approaches which can only, in the end, bring the whole nation to frustration and exhaustion.

The third imperative that makes long-range planning necessary is the dynamic pace of technological change, and the rise of research and innovation in all fields of functional work, as established techniques of competitive business enterprise. Very few substantial businesses today can expect to survive and grow without a dynamic plan for continuous innovation in products, processes, facilities, methods, organization, leadership, and all other aspects of the business. These innovations require early major investments in projects whose commercial maturity may not be reached for ten years or longer. Only the irresponsible manager would make such investments without a sound plan that takes into account not only competitive factors, but the whole range of changing conditions under which the future business will be conducted.

We must add to these three imperatives the historic, worldwide struggle for men's minds, in which the success or failure of the United States economy in the coming decades will be one critical factor.

The managers of individual businesses—and other individual organizations—in the United States must make the kind of responsible, long-range plans that will keep this country out ahead, as an example for all the world, so that the people in their disappointment will not turn to the state-planned economy that is at the heart of communist and socialist doctrine.

It is worthwhile, at this point, to review the advantages of decentralized or private planning over state planning. In a nation such as ours, where the political freedoms of the individual are protected, particularly the right to vote the government in or out of office, planning by government is always subject to considerations not necessarily related to the solution of the problem.

Long-range needs of the public are frequently subordinated to the individual politician's interpretation of his party's short-range needs for more votes. Government long-range plans are subject to change, as control shifts from one party to another or as parties strive for political advantages. Moreover, no single individual at any level of operations can be held personally accountable for the plans that are made.

The difficulty in making long-range plans in the

broad public interest is illustrated by the long frustration of the ardently debated ten-year highway program and the indecisive maneuvering about foreign-aid plans and the farm problem, almost entirely as a result of jockeying for partisan credit.

This is democracy, and its advantages outweigh its annoyances. But it is clear that leadership in long-range planning—especially where time periods longer than current election cycles are involved—needs to be sought in other quarters.

Another reason for the failure of state planning is the frequent tendency to make plans too small as well as too rigid. Great Britain lived by a philosophy of austerity for six years after World War II until the voters vetoed the plans of the Socialist-Labor planners and put them out of power. Even today, the Socialist legacy in England is causing an annual inflation of 7 to 10% which continues to bleed the British economy in spite of its surface symptoms of prosperity. Our own advocates of state planning in the United States noisily urged clinging to production controls, price ceilings, and other artificial limitations contrary to the desires of the citizens after World War II.

But the deepest reason why state planning has failed wherever it has been tried is that centralized bureaucratic control fails to provide either the information or the productivity that is provided by the United States' system of incentives and competition in a substantially free market. Where the market operates with comparative freedom, every citizen can exercise his personal choice—even the choice to do nothing. Where there is little freedom at the market place for people to decide what they want and what they will pay for it, one sees the artificial shortages or surpluses that plague every state-planned economy in the world, including the farm economy of the United States.

No amount of planning downward or outward by governments or corporations or individuals will ever produce the demand information or the right production of goods as to type or output, which is provided every day by the two-way communications process of the free market.

Limited, rigid, politically disjointed state planning cannot supply a vibrant and expanding economy for the United States, or satisfy the growing wants of awakened people anywhere. Just as the decentralization philosophy enhances flexibility and vitality in the large corporation, in the same way the decentralization of decision-making to the individual citizen provides the United States with the real ignition coil of its great forward drive.

MODERN BUSINESS PLANNING: A NEW DISCIPLINE

Modern business planning is a new and difficult discipline. Although a plan still properly embraces some combination of statistical data, forecasts, experimental methods in projection and prediction, and the essential ingredient of business judgment, its final validity depends on the long-range viewpoint which today's manager must develop as a habit of mind. Purposeful managers need to develop the capacity to influence rather than merely adapt to the business environment. With this viewpoint, the manager teaches himself to think of all his decisions in terms of the optimum in both the short- and the long-range consequences, and he is less likely to sacrifice tomorrow's great opportunities to a mere appearance of greater accomplishments today.

Too often, business plans have been no more than a straight-line extension of past trends, and have failed to take into account the probable success of current investments in research and innovation. This is why able businessmen are surprised more often by their successes than by their failures, and so are usually unable to capitalize opportunities that could have been anticipated. The manager who merely tries to keep his plans and policies up-to-date is already out-of-date. He must keep them up-to-the-future, where the objectives of the business will be achieved.

In planning ahead for the coming decade, a sound plan will assume the success of current business objectives. For example, let us assume doubled levels of electrical energy, where the average workman will have the energy equivalent of 500 men at his command. Let us assume the development of materials of vastly improved strength, light weight, and heat resistance. Let us assume that with automation and computer technology, the productivity of factories, offices, farms, and laboratories will be sharply increased.

In the economic area, let us assume a 1966 economy where the average man in the office or factory will have a vastly increased purchasing power available to buy goods and services and to invest in the ownership of the industry.

Socially, let us assume that by 1966 the American people have finally outgrown the shock and fears of depression psychology. Let us assume that they have become even more buoyant, more forward-looking, more willing to accept the risks and hazards of economic freedom in return for its abundant benefits. This can come about if managers and others do their part to help build greater public understanding of the full implications and opportunities of a free-market economy.

Such thrilling conditions seem highly probable 10 years hence, and sound planning can simultaneously envision and evaluate still other possibilities. Faced with such a vision of the future, the planner needs something far more than a straight-line extension of past trends; he has new conditions that call for new assumptions and new approaches to the business.

Bear in mind that the manager is not then rigidly limited to these assumptions about the future. Precisely because he has actually made some rational and specific assumptions, based on orderly data and information, he has a mechanism for later review and improvement of the plan as new facts and trends develop. For only if he clearly spells out what he anticipates will happen can he be sure of knowing when a plan needs to be reviewed and revised because actual events are diverging from his expectations.

By feeding in the results of new analyses from current operations, and by constantly adjusting his plans in the light of new developments, long-range planning thus becomes not a form of fortune-telling, but a progressive process that keeps the manager ahead of the needs of the business, working toward high but realistic objectives.

INFORMATION FOR DECISION-MAKING

The commitment to this new kind of long-range planning leads us to consider the next major area of challenge of professional managers: the organization and communication of information for decision-making, so that results can be anticipated, planned, achieved, and measured.

It would be difficult to state how much more information and knowledge is required to run a modern business than was the case in even the recent past. Perhaps the tremendous growth of the paper and communications industries offers a clue.

It appears that our technological progress to date has been bought at the price of increased complexity. One of my colleagues, a retired Vice President, Dr. Zay Jeffries, stated the challenge admirably when he said:

Our progress depends to a considerable extent on seeing to it that the simplifying processes move forward in approximate balance with the complicating processes. If this can be accomplished, then individuals with given ability can expect to go forward indefinitely without becoming casualties of their own complexities.

This achievement of balance between complicating and simplifying processes is the basic technological challenge in the field of managing.

It requires that managers apply work simplification to their own work no less than to the work of others.

In spite of the increased amount of information that is required to make decisions with a long-range viewpoint, the business manager needs to be able to grasp significant events as easily and as clearly as heretofore, and to speak and write about them with crispness.

BUSINESS MEASUREMENTS

In General Electric, one approach to this problem has been creative research into the area of business measurements. Like many other companies, General Electric has long felt a need for more exact measurements and standards of performance, not only to evaluate past results, but to provide a more accurate means for planning future activities and calculating business risks. The traditional measures of profits such as return on investment, turnover, and percent of net earnings to sales provide useful information. But they are hopelessly inadequate as measures to guide the manager's effectiveness in planning for the future of the business—the area where his decisions have the most important effects.

When General Electric undertook the thorough decentralization that I described in the previous lectures, the need for more realistic and balanced measurements became visibly more acute. For with the decentralization of operating responsibility and authority to more than a hundred local managerial teams, there was a need for common means of measuring these diverse business operations as to their short-range and long-range effectiveness.

A survey of the measurements already in use in the Company showed that they were at once too numerous, and yet not necessarily guiding decisions on a balanced basis toward the main objectives of the Company. Extensive review of the literature on business measurements produced helpful ideas but no ready-made system for General Electric's purposes.

Yet it was felt that, if a system of simple, common measurements could be devised they would have these important values to decentralized management:

1. Common measurements would provide all the managers of each component, and the individual contributors in the component, with means to measure and plan their own performance, so that their individual decisions could be made on the basis of knowledge and informed judgment.

2. Common measurements would provide each manager with a way of detecting deviations from established standards in time to do something about it —the feedback idea, in which current operations themselves provide a means of continuous adjustment of the operation.

3. Common measurements would provide a means of appraisal, selection, and compensation of men on the basis of objective performance rather than personality judgments, which is better for both the individual and the Company.

4. Common measurements would provide an important motivation for better performance, since they make clear on what basis the individual is to be measured and give him a way of measuring his own effectiveness.

5. Common measurements would simplify communications by providing common concepts and common language with which to think and talk about the business, especially in its quantitative aspects.

You will notice that all these points are directed at helping each decentralized manager and individual contributor measure and guide his own work, through self-discipline; they are not designed as a way for others to "second-guess" the manager of a component or the workers in his component. When measurements are designed primarily for the "boss" rather than for the man himself, they tend to lose their objectivity and frequently become instruments of deception.

An adequate system of common measurements, moreover, would have the additional advantage of providing the Company's executives with a way of evaluating performance in some hundred different businesses without becoming involved in the operational details of each of them.

With these incentives to do pioneering into the field of business measurements, the Company established a Measurements Project in 1952. The project is still in operation, and its method of organization may be of interest to you.

The project is now in Measurements Service, a permanent organization component in the Accounting Services. To study a particular problem of measurement, a study team is gathered of men from different functions and departments of the Company who have knowledge to contribute to the study. These individuals are detached from regular work for the period of the study, to devote adequate time to the work of the study team. Each study team is under the direction of a Consultant from the Measurements Service component.

General Electric makes frequent use of this type of study team or task force to work on research projects of Company-wide importance. This not only provides a simple means to assemble special talents for special projects, but provides the participants with new experiences at the corporate level which contribute greatly to their self-development.

After a set of first principles was established, the over-all Measurements Project was segregated into three major sub-projects to develop the following:

Operational measurements, to measure the results of a decentralized profit-and-loss business component as a whole;

Functional measurements, to measure the work of engineering, manufacturing, marketing, finance, employee and plant community relations, and legal components of the organization;

And measurements of the work of managing as such—planning, organizing, integrating, and measuring itself.

Work on the first phase of the project—the development of operational measurements—is well advanced. The fundamental concept in this work is the identification of what are called "Key Result Areas" by which it is possible to measure the balanced performance of a business as a whole. A Key Result Area is one that meets this test:

"Will continued failure in this area prevent attainment of managerial responsibility for advancing General Electric as a leader in a strong, competitive economy, even though results in all other Key Result Areas are good?"

This evaluation has produced the following eight Key Result Areas:

1. Profitability.
2. Market position.
3. Productivity, or the effective utilization of human, capital, and material resources.
4. Product leadership.
5. Personnel development.
6. Employee attitudes.

7. Public responsibility.
8. Balance between short-range and long-range goals.

In each of these Key Result Areas, the Measurements Project is formulating common indexes of performance, but is not concerned with developing common standards. For example, rate of return on investment is an *index* common to all businesses but the *standard* in terms of this index might be 20% for one business, 25% for another, and 30% for a third. The standards of performance as well as the weighting of each of the Key Result Areas must be established for each business by its operating managers according to the nature of the particular business at a particular point on its own growth curve.

The development of such measurements, and of equivalent, applicable indexes in each functional area, is not complete or more than well underway. When completed, the resulting measurements offer no route to automatic decision-making. Measurements are designed to maximize, not minimize, judgment. They provide a valuable tool to help managers and individual contributors make decisions based upon a greater amount of factual knowledge. Thus they can help evaluate choices among alternative risks, but the man has to make the decision himself, and at the time it is needed.

THE COMMUNICATIONS CHALLENGE

The development of measurements is important, but it is only one part of the immense problem of organizing and communicating the necessary information required to operate a large, decentralized organization to achieve defined objectives and known common purposes.

This deep problem of communication is not solved by providing more volume of data for all concerned, or even by faster accumulation and transmittal of conventional data, or by wider distribution of previously existing data, or through holding more conferences. Indeed, the belief that such measures will meet the communications challenge is probably one of the great fallacies in business and managerial thinking.

What is required, instead, is a far more penetrating and orderly study of the business in its entirety to discover what specific information is needed at each particular position in view of the decisions to be made there.

OPERATIONS RESEARCH AND SYNTHESIS

One promising approach to this problem is the discipline that has now become known as operations research and synthesis. Operations research first came into prominence during World War II, when it was applied with great success to such involved problems as analyzing and predicting enemy submarine attack patterns, and working out the most efficient and economical form of defense.

Since that time, a number of companies, including General Electric, have been studying ways to apply and extend operations research philosophy and techniques—including the techniques of mathematics, formal logic, and scientific method—to the analysis, measurement, and anticipation of business activities.

These techniques will be helpful in dealing with such matters in each of the business functions. Their original applications for fact-finding, or research as such, are being amplified to discover patterns and principles from the facts, which is synthesis. Such principles and patterns should have value in anticipating and guiding the future course of the enterprise.

Those who are studying operations research and

synthesis are increasingly convinced that its greatest values may thus lie in helping both the general manager and functional managers to see the business as a whole, to plan its course more confidently, and to communicate such plans more clearly.

The approach requires that each decentralized business be viewed as a rational process or system, whose assumptions, objectives, and patterns of operation can be productively subjected to scientific analysis. From such analysis, with the aid of mathematical and scientific techniques, the manager is able to synthesize a progressively clearer "model" of the business which will enable him and his associates to measure and guide its progress with steadily greater accuracy and consistency.

A word of caution is also in order here, as was cited in noting that better measurements aid, but do not replace, judgment. To adopt a system or approach that relies primarily on statistics could easily foster a dangerous tendency to assume that anything which cannot be expressed numerically does not actually exist. Such a highly theoretical approach could lead to excessive rigidity, and to overlooking many of the most important factors, especially the human factors. Neither research nor the manager can ignore such human factors.

General Electric is steadily building experience in operations research and synthesis studies, and is constantly re-evaluating its possible long-term usefulness. It is a field of great promise, and its use in the specific situations to which it has been applied has encouraged the Company to continue exploring the possibilities of its future success as another significant aid in managerial decision-making.

CRITICAL AREA: HUMAN MOTIVATIONS

Now, finally, I should like to explore with you the most critical area of all, the area of human motivations.

Why do people work?

What satisfactions and rewards do they expect to find in their work?

How can they find the sense of full and responsible participation in an enterprise, the motivation that brings out their full talents, enthusiasm, and performance in working toward common objectives?

These are perplexing challenges. They lie close to the heart of the industrial society. They will never be wholly solved, but patient and sympathetic study will always yield new understanding.

Some of General Electric's most fruitful research

in this area was begun in 1948, and continues every year. A survey was conducted among the employees as to what they liked and what they did not like about their work. Their replies were subjected to careful analysis, and out of the study emerged certain qualities that an employee wants to find in his position with General Electric. The order of importance varies with each individual and with the local conditions. They are as follows:

Rewarding associations on the job, or a sense of belonging.

Important and significant work, or a sense of purpose.

Full information.

Good pay and other material benefits.

Good working conditions.

Good managers.

Steady work.

A fair chance to get ahead.

Respectful treatment.

There is nothing startling in this prescription, yet it speaks deep truths to the thoughtful student of human motivations. Each of these categories presents almost endless opportunities to the manager who recognizes that human resources are ultimately the resources that count most deeply in an enterprise.

It has become the Company's practice to design into its positions these nine desirable qualities, in return for the skill, care, effort, teamwork, and attendance on the part of the employee who fills each position.

As I have tried to indicate in the previous lectures, the achievement of such powerful human motivations and satisfactions throughout the entire organizations starts with the very philosophy of management: the decentralization philosophy that recognizes the dignity and capacity of each individual. It is implemented in the structuring of the organization, and of each position in the organization, so that each position has its own responsibility and authority. It is implemented in the climate that prevails—and that is deliberately created—in each organizational component, and in each man-to-manager relationship. It is implemented in the ethical behavior, and therefore the ethical beliefs, that guide a company in its work toward honorable and responsible objectives.

In this matter of providing the right human motivations, it is not enough merely to have good intentions, or even a sound philosophy. The opportunities in human motivation can be subjected to research, and new practices and approaches can be developed that turn good intentions into actualities.

ECONOMIC INCENTIVES

As a concrete example of this, General Electric began, five years ago, a thorough study into the matter of financial and economic incentives. The purpose of this continuing study is not only to develop integrated compensation practices that recognize the distinctive contributions of individuals in every component of the organization; the study includes more important basic research into the nature and effect of the economic motivations, their relationships to other motivations that may be more deeply significant, and ways to express these relationships in the practices of the Company so that they provide optimum incentives and rewards for all employees.

At the present time, General Electric utilizes four principal types of financial incentive:

First, there are wages and salaries, in which the Company tries to establish fair compensation levels for satisfactory performance, position by position and community-by-community. This is done both for positions subject to collective bargaining and for others. For the salaried employees who are exempt from overtime provisions of the Fair Labor Standards Act, the Company has developed an integrated structure of 28 position levels which are applied throughout the organization. Each of these position levels has a certain salary range, and each "exempt" salaried position in the Company, from the beginner to the President, is identified with one of these levels. Thus the Company has a rational and balanced salary structure, but the responsibility and authority to determine at which level a position should be located, and how much salary an individual receives in the range of that position level, has been decentralized. It is interesting to note as an evidence of decentralization that the typical General Electric department manager now has as much authority over salaries as the President formerly had.

The second form of financial incentive is what are known as "employee benefit programs," such as pensions, medical and life insurance, and the like. In this field, as I have indicated in earlier lectures, General Electric has long pioneered. It should be noted that the Company has only one system of employee benefit programs, and it applies across the Company from the man in the factory to the Officers of the Company.

The third form of financial incentive is what is known as incentive compensation, which provides almost 2,000 key employees with a variable additional payment determined at year-end to reflect the individual's actual achievement of both short-range and long-range objectives during the past year.

The fourth form of financial incentive is a "restricted" stock option plan which encourages key managers and other leading professional employees to have a greater long-term interest and risk in the Company's over-all results. As another example of the Company's thorough decentralization, nearly 1,000 qualified key employees are participating in the stock option plan, and the number can be increased to 1,200 through present share-owner authorization. Such financial incentives are important, of course, in attracting and holding outstanding leadership, in building the value of the share owners' investment, and in assuring long-range decisions that are in the public interest.

These various financial incentives are constantly under study, and research and experiments continue in order to determine the relationships of such incentives to employee performance and satisfaction. Since such factors will always be dynamic in a dynamic organization and in a changing social structure, the study and change will, of course, never end. The important thing is that a given structure of financial motivation—or any other practice—be kept from becoming so fixed and rigid that it defeats rather than advances the purposes of the organization and the society of which it is part.

While I have concentrated here on financial incentives as an example to show the concrete nature of the Company's efforts at motivation, you will realize from the points made in all three lectures that the non-material motivations are the deeper, more critical determinants. From the basic philosophy of organizing and managing to the personal relationships between man and manager, General Electric is trying to develop a climate in which each individual in the enterprise can constructively translate personal aspirations that are important to him into performance and results important to our customers, owners, suppliers, distributors, and the general public.

There is not time, in these lectures, even to discuss many other areas of vital opportunity that lie before the professional manager as he looks at a future of accelerating change. For each company, in each industry, these challenges will take specific forms that call for individually tailored solutions.

The examples that I have cited, in these three McKinsey Lectures, represent only General Electric's approach to General Electric's opportunities, and are not suggested as directly transferable solutions to the operations of other companies.

Beyond these challenges that are, in a sense, internal to each company, there are the challenges of external environment that face all companies.

THE ECONOMIC CLIMATE

The plans of managers and the efforts of all the participants in the enterprise can come to optimum fruition only in an economic, political, and social environment which is favorable to the full play of organized energies and skills that are now available to the American economy. This will require deep understanding and conviction on the part of the citizens of this country, and indeed of the whole world in the long run, as to how the American concepts of responsible freedom in all matters—including economic matters—can bring new levels of spiritual as well as material attainments for everyone.

The professional manager cannot assume that such understanding and conviction exist on the part of his fellow citizens. He needs to study these issues for himself, and to be articulate in every situation where he can make a contribution to public understanding. He needs to influence others to do so.

This will mean facing up to some difficult business questions with broad political and social overtones. For example, what are the ultimate implications of efficiency?

A well-managed company may become so sensitive in anticipating the wants of the American people, and so efficient in serving them, that a large portion of the customers may decide they want to buy a given product from that one company. In other words, a company may in a given year earn a major share of the market through the wholly ethical and legal means of providing the best product value available, by a wide margin, in a given product line.

There are critics who feel that this is not good for the American people. They feel that it is the duty of the government to repudiate the will of the people as so expressed at the market place, and somehow limit or tax or frighten the successful company into being less successful.

What is the duty of the professional manager in such cases? Surely he should not hold back innovations out of fear, or raise his prices to shelter less efficient competitors. It seems to me that the first duty of a company is to serve its customers just as well as it knows how. The laws of the land can and do provide protection against monopoly, but in a free-market situation where monopoly does not exist, it is the customer, by his free choice at the market place, who determines the size, profitability, and growth of a company.

In the fast-growing electrical industry, where General Electric competes actively with hundreds of competitors in many product lines, the dynamics of competition serve both as incentive and regulator on the growth and profitability of any company. There are so many opportunities for new products, or new features for old products, or new approaches that can, in a few short years, change the market position of many competitors, that young and energetic companies are always coming into being or rising into prominence. With its philosophy of decentralization, General Electric simultaneously tries to improve its competitive effectiveness and to achieve the sensitivity to customer and public interest which comes from having decision-making authority at the point where these interests are most intimately affected.

The progress of a company must certainly be measured by more than "dollars and cents." We need to look to other goals and longer-range objectives that perhaps involve the welfare of the nation several business generations after us, and the preservation of a competitive-enterprise system in the true sense. If business leaders build well and securely today, they will insure economic strength for their companies; but unless that strength is used prudently in the balanced best interests of all, business will run into trouble.

I have spoken of what in my judgment are some of the challenges that the professional managers and their other professional colleagues in the modern corporation have no choice but to explore deeply, objectively, and creatively. This must be done if they are to fulfill their responsibilities to their companies, to the society they serve, and to themselves as individuals who have voluntarily undertaken precisely these responsibilities.

What I have been trying to stress in these lectures is the importance of each manager trying rationally to anticipate the conditions and the opportunities that will face his company in the future. Then, through research and through forward-looking decisions, he can prepare for and meet these coming challenges with strength and purpose.

This is not the work of the manager alone; it is

the work of every forward-looking man and woman in the enterprise.

SHARING THE VISION: A CHALLENGE TO LEADERSHIP

Any sensitive observer must agree that the human potential in business has never been fully unleashed. The great dream of the professional manager is that some day, he will find a way to share with his associates a mutually deep vision of what a truly inspired human organization can achieve. How can he build this managerial vision on all that they, as well as he, have to contribute to its formulation? How can he help every man and woman in the organization find a sense of true participation in working toward high and noble objectives that will bring everyone a sense of pride and satisfaction?

I confess, this is one of the deepest desires of my life: to bring about such unity of purpose throughout the General Electric organization.

These thoughts bring us again to that philosophy of management that was discussed in the previous lecture, the philosophy that recognizes the freedom, and the dignity, and the capacity of each individual, and eagerly asks for what he alone can bring to the organization.

I am convinced that there is no such thing as the common man. Each of us is an uncommon man. Each of us has some distinctive and individual contribution that he alone can make.

When the professional manager at every echelon of the organization recognizes this, and cherishes it as his most deeply held belief about his fellow men, then he has found the clue to leadership in the American society. It is leadership of this kind that will determine whether the way of freedom will be the way of the world.

APPENDIX

GENERAL ELECTRIC
COMPANY
OBJECTIVES

1. To carry on a diversified, growing, and profitable world-wide manufacturing business in electrical apparatus, appliances, and supplies, and in related materials, products, systems, and services for industry, commerce, agriculture, government, the community, and the home.

2. To lead in research in all fields of science and in all areas of work relating to the business, including managing as a distinct and a professional kind of work, so as to assure a constant flow of new knowledge and of resultant useful and valuable new products, processes, services, methods, and organizational patterns and relationships; and to make real the Company theme that "Progress Is Our Most Important Product."

3. To operate each business venture to achieve its own

favorable customer acceptance and profitable results; especially by planning the product line or services through decentralized operating management, on the basis of continuing research as to markets, customers, distribution channels, and competition, and as to product or service features, styling, price range, and performance for the end user, taking appropriate business risks to meet changing customer needs and to offer customers timely choice in product and service availability and desirability.

4. To design, make, and market all Company products and services with good quality and with inherent customer value, at fair prices for such quality and value.

5. To build public confidence and continuing friendly feeling for products and services bearing the Company's name and brands through sound, competitive advertising, promotion, selling, service, and personal contacts.

6. To provide good jobs, wages, working conditions, work satisfactions, and opportunities for advancement conducive of most productive performance and also the stablest possible employment, all in exchange for loyalty, initiative, skill, care, effort, attendance, and teamwork on the part of employees—the contributions of individual employees that result in "Value to the Company" and for which the employee is being paid.

7. To manage the enterprise for continuity and flow of progress, growth, profit, and public service through systematic selection and development of competent managerial personnel for effective leadership through persuasive managerial planning, organizing, integrating, and measuring for best utilization of both the human and material resources

of the business; using a clear and soundly designed organization structure, and clearly expressed objectives and policies, as a vehicle for freeing the abilities, capacities, resourcefulness, and initiative of all managers, other professional workers and all employees for dynamic individual efforts and teamwork, encouraged by incentives proportionate to responsibilities, risks, and results.

8. To attract and retain investor capital in amounts adequate to finance the enterprise successfully through attractive returns as a continuing incentive for wide investor participation and support; securing such returns through sound business and economic research, forecasting, planning, cost management, and effectively scheduled turnover of all assets of the enterprise.

9. To cooperate both with suppliers and also with distributors, contractors, and others facilitating distribution, installation, and servicing of Company products, so that Company efforts are constructively integrated with theirs for mutually effective public service and competitive, profitable progress.

10. To adapt Company policies, products, services, facilities, plans, and schedules to meet continuously, progressively, foresightedly, imaginatively, and voluntarily the social, civic, and economic responsibilities commensurate with the opportunities afforded by the size, success, and nature of the business and of public confidence in it as a corporate enterprise.